*Southern Messenger Poets*

DAVE SMITH, EDITOR

Joy in the Morning

poems

Claude Wilkinson

LOUISIANA STATE UNIVERSITY PRESS

Baton Rouge

2004

Designer: Amanda McDonald Scallan
Typeface: Whitman
Printer and binder: Thomson-Shore, Inc.

Library of Congress Cataloging-in-Publication Data
Wilkinson, Claude.
  Joy in the morning : poems / Claude Wilkinson.
    p. cm. — (Southern messenger poets)
  ISBN 0-8071-3005-2 (alk. paper) — ISBN 0-8071-3006-0 (pbk. : alk. paper)
  I. Title. II. Series.
 PS3573.I44183J695 2004
 811'.54—dc22

                                                                        2004005185

The author offers grateful acknowledgment to the following publications, in which some of the poems herein orig-
inally appeared, sometimes in a different form: *Chattahoochee Review:* "Arkabutla Reservoir, Au revoir," "Flying
Blind," "The Grace of Dreams," "Grail," "Hope against Hope," "Idea of Beauty," "Mixed Blessing," "Mourning Song,"
"Summer's End"; *Colorado North Review:* "Golden Years"; *Georgetown Review:* "Staples"; *Mississippi Poetry
Journal:* "Elegy," "Imperfect Works"; *A New Song:* "Words to Live By"; *Old Hickory Review:* "Art," "Boy and Dog,"
"Music"; *Oxford American:* "Cape Cod Evening, 1939," "The Enduring Night"; *Poem:* "Lately," "Selah"; Red Owl:
"Joy in the Morning," "Manna"; *Sonoma Mandala Literary Review:* "Ritual"; *South Dakota Review:* "Pastoral";
Southern Review: "The Barbershop," "A Fable," "The Family of Bro. Cliff Phillips," "Melancholy," "The Persistence
of Memory"; *Terminus:* "A Gift of Venison," "Parable, Late October"; *Xavier Review:* "Oldies"; *Yalobusha Review:*
"Nocturne."

CONTENTS

Weeping may endure for a night,
but joy comes in the morning.
—PSALM 30:5

Joy in the Morning

THE ENDURING NIGHT

after a painting by Michael Crespo

Still in the beginning
before order and purpose,
without cushions of moss
or tumbling rivers,
without swallows dropping
from palm fronds into flight,

moon and rabbit
are stacked like
porcelain objets d'art, float
as if models for creation
in the black chiffon of space.

Certainly this is that time
that Roethke meant
when he said, "I weep
for what I'm like
when I'm alone."

Moon, rabbit, dark.

Who among us hasn't stood
in the same empty
square of canvas,
as unhappy as God, overlooking
swaths of new-mown grass
and shell pink azaleas,
unmoved even by lagoons of stars?

Who hasn't blended into
the one infinite night,
and with raucous crickets,
a death owl's quavering whistle,
waited for silver morning
to bleed through?

FLYING BLIND

Yes, through umbrellas
of Queen Anne's lace, this
gloriously orgasmic earth,
two redbirds, the buff question
with its vivid answer
half a beat behind,
sling in front of me,
what might've been the end
in a poof of feathers
against a headlight.

Montague and Capulet,
they've crossed eros
into consuming quest
where they either
first impale themselves
on errant thorn, or
he overtakes her
by a quick, fiery shower,
and they become of one mind
in redbud or nettle.

No doubt somewhere, at least
one other, near Biloxi
or Brussels perhaps,
having witnessed the passion
of birds in spring,
dreams for himself
a simpler, less possible
course, of trusting
only the needle
of his flesh.

MIXED BLESSING

Out from under
a kerosene-soaked mound
of brush and thistle,
my last three springs
of grappling with honeysuckle,
rose the tussle of something
dewy, animal, nuzzling deeper
into rotting pine straw.

I stood, hating to let slip
that stillness of air,
then giving in
to plumb the lattice
of blackberry cane, through ivy
and powder of goldenrod
to where they were.

Four spitting images.

Two as yellowish
as the phantom tomcat
that comes like a gardener,
as regularly as moonlight,
to spray our compass
of saplings and shrubbery,
and two the same mottled silver
as their hunter-gatherer mother.

Until I scooped them out,
the sum of their lives
had been nipples and comfort.
But who is ever more than
a stone's throw from suffering,
a speck on an x-ray,
some confusion in the stool?

If their weak, opalescent eyes
missed the crackling blaze of home
surging toward sky,
and mother upon her return,
as rigid as Niobe
before the charred clump,
then at least this
could be counted joy.

Even now, I can feel her
leaving, coming back
every hour or so,
each time more puzzled
over fuming ash,
no longer able to trust
the same hungry mewing
just across the yard.

No matter where I moved them,
she still couldn't believe
they were hers.
So again I was working
to heal or feed someone
or something back
to the world of the living,
as I'd worked with my mother
while she waned and recovered
and waned till it was over.

Again, the soft cross
of rabbits, ground squirrels,
nestlings I'd found,
tended and lost down the years
was pulled through the knot
of my heart, while these new ones'
tiny, sandpaper tongues
smacked and strangled
at a futile concoction
of cat's milk
in an eyedropper, on fingertips.

Behold the law
of mysterious ways: beyond
this obligation of grace
is another season's nodding
of columbine, another life
being spared from one fire
for the next.

THE GRACE OF DREAMS

With all the possibilities to dream of,
why not that picture of Rousseau's where
lions peek like astonished kittens
through passionflower and fern, where trees
festooned with monkeys and fruit
surround two nudes: one, earthier,
almost hidden in understory,
pipes a horn as if a muse
for the other's desire; and the other,
as fair as sunlight, reclined
on settee, beckoning to come,
if we can, into her perfect peace?

That, or some other green destiny
blooming at the edge
of my mind, and yet one vision
recurs in biblical fashion,
as when something as occult
as seven gaunt cattle
rising from the river to eat
their fat sisters
grazing in a meadow
warned the king of Egypt
that seven bountiful years
would be swallowed by seven lean.

One soldier's dream of a barley loaf
spilling down the mountainside
and leveling a Midianite tent
spelt the force of Gideon's sword—
as usual, the trial
with a grain of promise.
So maybe even in my field
of only tall bleached grass
and its single leafless scrub,
without breeze or sound
and where nothing ever happens,
hides the favor of the Lord.

IMPERFECT WORKS

What good is one
more anonymous bug
scuffling to right itself
for a brief, empty future?
A bunting with its purple
satin head and shot
with green, yellow, red,
frantic to be lovely again
in a paean of dogwood,
that I could understand.

All such a drab
nodule of life
is likely to do is try
another wall too slick
and steep, or get
eaten by any of
a thousand things,
or be crushed underfoot.

But then, even it
surely must cherish
some communion and urge,
its privilege to keep
messing up, so I stoop
and lean toward it,
like Michelangelo's God.

BOY AND DOG

O that you'd led on,
　　wagging your wavy flag,
　　　finding our way
　　　　through tall redtop,

under fences
　　and onto others'
　　　land. Had I only known
　　　　of that last day

you'd somehow
　　drag back
　　　after weeks, flies brooding
　　　　in your wounds, of all

the mornings I'd waken
　　missing someone,
　　　how soon I'd abandon
　　　　the wisdom of skimming stones,

I too would've
　　plunged
　　　into each creek we found,
　　　　wallowed deliciously in sunny meadows,

and followed your nose
　　toward every chance
　　　of happiness till we were so impossibly
　　　　lost, no voice could call us home.

ART

"There's an art to it,"
Mama said, smiling, years later
when I asked, thinking of her

teaching me to scatter feed,
how gently we must handle
the chicks. "All that winding

and swinging other people do,
all you need are these three
fingers," holding up her index,

middle and thumb, as if
to throw me a curve.
"A quick snap, jerk

and quarter-twist." And I
remembered vermilion combs,
glassy eyes of Dominique,

Leghorn, Orpington, cupped
in her hand, their dumb,
shocked bodies flopping

into, around us, jetting blood
and feathers across the dusty yard.
Soon after, there was a last

flutter, then absolute quiet,
heads were dropped, and supper
fetched by the shank.

GRAIL

Every Christmas, while webs
of breath shivered from me,
I bore the icy lesson
of faith: that is, to wait
and keep waiting.

Under a temple
of sycamore and locust,
the flurry-glittered cedars,
I hoped for something different
from an ordinary broadcast of stars,
for the already dark sky
to pitch completely black,
except for one remarkable fire—
a shepherd's sign
for me to rise and follow.

What I wanted
was to be changed
from child to a giver
of omens and dreams,
to be led along the fence line
beyond our few head of cows
clamped together against harm,
through paths of burdock,
into a cove filled
with as clear a beacon
as those for Saul and Monet,

some place where
I could've listened
to the sound of
a hoot owl's swoop
down from its tower
through ripples of wind,
or for anything else
even slightly like
the shuffling of angels' wings.

OLDIES

Before my starry eyes
again, our dusty routes
swirl behind us
in a honeyed mist settling
over walls of kudzu,
with me on the shotgun side
of Fred's '65 Ford,
its chrome wheels flashing,
piercing the dark like flares.

Down gravel lanes
we cruised, enough
cheap brew between us,
and the Ford's pipes
rumbling as richly
as a whole week's pay.

Song from ditchwater
and sweet gums was almost
as loud a hullabaloo
as the volume
of our platters:
the ones that crooned
nearly foolproof ways
of getting girls we hoped for,
dreamed of, drove toward as if
they were bull's-eyes. Everywhere
fireflies dipped and swayed
to summer's metronome.

How quickly what's lost
can become the zenith of a life.
Then how dear we hold
the hastily scrawled,
yellowed and crumbling
"Luv U 4-ever,"
our memories of the last dance.

Bits we think we've forgotten
drift through the years
till notes and moments
are freshly matched, till
all we care about
is tapping the present
to oblivion, a scrapbook
of harvest moons,
keeping time, being
4-ever at the bright
hub of youth.

CAPE COD EVENING, 1939

Oil on canvas, and yet,
even in Hopper's aloof collie,
its sorrel and white coat
so fluffed and burnished
in South Truro light, the soliloquy
of anguish seems beyond
what anything could take.

As if from the insoluble blue corner
of balsam trees, shadow settles
on a cropped, white facade.
Mixtures of violet and turquoise
are scumbled like bruises
under each clapboard, over drawn curtains,
into the doorway's etched glass.

A stoutish, middle-aged woman
with arms folded
across her sea green dress,
leans against the house's bay window,
her eyes fixed somewhere
in the billowing chaos
of dry, sunlit grass.

In dark trousers and pale muslin shirt
with sleeves rolled up above
muscles of hard work,
the man, fumbling
with a tuft of grass,
sits on their stoop
a couple of chasmal feet away.

What a world to be reminded of,
ordained to, with nothing
to soften this onset of autumn,
no amaryllis nor rose of heaven—
only the blond, irretrievable evening
that hearts spend holding
whatever is crying out to be said.

PASTORAL

Remembering the days of pear and plum
and my feeding them to our cows by hand
is heavy effort, a painful command.
After decades, I recall names of some
like Angus and Muley, the season's hum
of cicadas, songbirds, a holy strand
that wound me into the calm of the land
till dreaded mornings when rough men would come
in trucks for hauling and change everything.
Stumbling wild-eyed up ramps, cows couldn't know
their gift of paths and sweet hands was over.
Some mercy shone in those we were keeping,
but this was our way. Then times would follow
when others ambled up through the clover.

LATELY

Light skips over the pond,
just as when my uncle showed
me how to cast between

snags of willow
and wait for a bob,
wait for a yank.

Then our few checkers
and bottle caps being
emptied onto a board

clatter to mind like clumsy ghosts.
Still, when he'd finished freezing
one January in the VA Hospital

after another weeklong drunk
there seemed so little left:
an echo of chuckling

at the punch line from
his favorite dirty riddle
about why a dog raises

its leg to pee; a brand-new
plug of Apple Sun Cured
atop the whatnot; his pump

action 12-gauge slanted
in a cold, poky closet
hopelessly off plumb.

ELEGY

Partridge yet call
   from under the hill,
      but our vegetable patch,
         my mother's crepe myrtle

and the house
   are finished.
      Besides bitterweed,
         there's the memory

of dirt daubers
   singing in the walls
      all summer long,
         winter rain on our

tin roof.
   Can anyone say
      what sky and lake
         and flowers lose

in time's grave design?
   Renoir would have it,
      "Pain passes, but beauty remains."
         In other words, there's always,

for those who
   never hold days
      wildly enough, some
         paradise not faded away.

THE FAMILY OF BRO. CLIFF PHILLIPS

Like the hollow taste
of communion bread, his name
lingered under "Sick and Shut In,"
above the last-ditch "Request for Prayer,"
where his family
now waits to be healed—
lists that are always inserted between
pearls of a revived, better life
and something as wondrous
as a frieze of lilies.

Here among sacred constants—
our responsive reading;
ministry of music;
ministry of giving;
ministry of another Sunday morning's Word—
he had clung on through
the pink apple blossoms of spring,
through June beetles' clumsy crashings
into carports and arbors,
almost through the drab descent
of summer into autumn again.

What does one pray
for those left behind
in the twinkling we all move toward?
That they should
or shouldn't remember
unfettered knuckles, the promise
in his flickering gaze?

Surely it's that they'll lose themselves
in a river of shamrock,
be blessed by
white arrows of sea birds
lunging then lifting
through radiant schools of fish.

What other choice have we
than to be made whole
with a coneflower's purple alms,
while it's yet too soon
to be comforted by
God's ineffable voice?

RITUAL

Shadow and moonlight mingle
on the field where an easy ax
of wings falls toward scurrying.

A stray overturns my garbage can.
Night's bookmark lifted, every means
to its end resumes. Beyond

the stiff scent of evergreen,
this window from where I'm reading
a universe, one is bowed by

her limit of dark, lonely hours,
ends that never meet, the pregnant
daughter, and even if just

for a moment, needs to get drunk
on Jesus. Another fenced in
with vital white noise, rises

to refill his highball glass.
Yet stars tell enough beautiful lies
of peace being still, that by and by,

I draw the curtains, feeling
utterly helpless and blessed,
hoping the mouse or whatever

wasn't a mother with babies,
that tomorrow, when the first rays
break, the garbage won't smell.

MANNA

Once in winter,
dropped on my porch,
a small torch of feathers
lay as red as ever,
the last of its strength
clenched into fists,
and as in those paintings
of Icarus falling, with one
brilliant, extended wing.

For the rest of the day,
nothing else touched me—
not huffing trucks
on distant roads,
nor a gray ache in the wind,
not the murmuration of starlings
that made their way
through freezing drizzle,
that came and vanished
into ragged trees.

And again, the spring
I was losing my father,
a metallic green beetle,
effulgent and still,
jeweled the dull step
at my door.

From one angle,
it blushed bluer than Nile,
from another purplish,
and yet another, as golden
as anything on earth.

As the beetle's colors changed
under patterns of light,
the usual questions arose:
How do we mourn for something
so wondrously cruel?
What, in the end,
are our bodies worth? If
this is heaven's offering
today, from what hunger
am I being saved?

ARKABUTLA RESERVOIR, AU REVOIR

Evening's exhibition of pastels falls into
        murky crescent glow
that cascades over us as we sit

        upon bleachers
of white stones alongshore, looking out on
        all but invisible

groves and a distant puncture of red
        warning aircraft.
Then, there's nothing but the odd harangue

        of a lone duck,
lake lapping below our confession of mistakes
        and our promise

to go separate ways. We listen as a drunken
        duet of boys
come and dive in, then slosh out and leave

        when their girlfriends
refuse to go skinny-dipping. Then, nothing again
        but the ebb and flow of waves

till your hand finds one of its ancient paths
        to some secret part of me
to show me a shooting star whipping out

        of eternity, across
molten blue night. You rest it there
        like a sextant

in my back, fingering between my shoulders
        the wonderful, risky curves
of Andromeda or Virgo. Who remembers or cares?

O Paradise!
Who has ever really cared once wrapped
            in this shawl

of impractical light? But if only you and I
            could turn for a moment
from such an arc of bright beginnings

            and pray
to some near, swift angel of interruption
            like the mosquito perhaps,

praising our bodies with her bloodthirsty aria,
            pray for the comic relief
of another invasion of amorous boys, that

            our halcyon
unlatch its wings, rise in thunderhead and spray,
            for anything that will keep us

from trying the same miserable lies a new,
            innumerable time,
for the world to be easier than this.

THE BARBERSHOP

With the jawbones of asses,
we enter rank and file to join
shaggy allies already thick
in their smoke of fretting and cigarettes.
From huddles of two or three
scattered against the walls,
politics, bits of debts or sex
rise and fall through the drone
of freshly oiled shears, a phone
ringing with appointments
till someone's magic phrase
knots us into one heroic chorus.

As the Romeos among us
finish laying waste
women's arts of controlling a man,
another is summoned to our inner sanctum
of attention to be cropped,
shaven, anointed with pomade.

After the gardener makes me vow to try
his prescription for killing nut grass,
I overhear one's smothered scheme
for cheating with a girl half his age.
When the farmers settle
that one's indifferent bull is strictly
a liability, that at eight hundred pounds
and pizzle unbroken, he should
be more than willing to fill a pasture
with calves, we conquer what remains
of crouched philistines till nothing
is left but that utopian lull
we fear most, till the last of us tramples out
over the dingy fleece of our strength.

A GIFT OF VENISON

Among the catacombs
of a tattered davenport,
hood off an old T-bird,
garden tools balanced into cones,
the jumble of plastic flamingos
hedging every step,
and berry-colored wasps
dizzy with spring,
Benjamine, my friend
since high school,
props open a freezer.

Beneath milk light,
the vapor of blood
rushes from neatly wrapped
saddle and sausage
of a spike buck and doe.
As he describes aim and blaze
that took each of them,
his brown, calloused hands
dig for clean packages,
brush away sequins of frost.

I look out at
his bed of yarrow,
the thundercloud plum—
a glorious cabala hinting
that the knowledge of flora
is the beginning of wisdom.

I want to say how incredibly
graceful and dumb deer are,
that I've watched them
put their minds to crossing
a hundred yards away, not yielding
for slices of barbwire
or glittering semis,
to tell him of a poet
who's written wonderful lines
on catching their shapes
backlit by morning,
tipping over rows
to nibble sweet corn.

But Ben goes on, wistful
about the eight-point
he'd somehow missed,
and with palms supine
as though before an altar,
offers me an ivory square
and a marble-hard cylinder,
for all the world like
kind geometries of fate.

"Maybe your stand shook,
maybe next time," I say,
my fingers stinging so
with the cold
that I can hardly believe
calendar-green hawthorn
beside his deep blue porch,
a marvelous stag still jostling
through lively shrubs
of willow and maple
and the first aspen shoots.

NOCTURNE

Between huge volunteer
catalpa trees,
before I'd heard
my father's death rattle,
his spirit scaling
a cage of bones,
stumbling back
to his chest
for another
rough breath,

I stood listening
in the dusky
throng of peepers,
to owls hooked high above,
swiveling incantations
over their realm of food.

What were powdery blows
of candleflies
in the face of all
the moon unveiled?
What was death then
but the twitching
crease of fur
draped in an owl's
crooked beak, or news
from some other hill?

And now, whatever voice
from the orchard grass,
whatever sparks
aligning themselves,
all the suffocating odors
of flowers summon
those last dark hours

I spent bedside
squeezing my father's
nearly translated hand.

"What bird is that singing?"
and "Things okay,
between you and me?"
he'd return through
a haze of Ativan to ask.

I gritted and bore
every memory
I'd tried to forget,
how much of a burden
I'd often felt
unless something was to be done,
a fence repaired,
or a stray tracked
and brought home.

I'd remember only
how on a summer's night
under our canvas of stars,
I clambered onto his lap
and touched his unshaven face
while he croaked
my favorite refrain
into the shadows
of flame-red cannas
and mimosas lavender
by moonlight:
Just over in the glory land,
I'll join the happy angel band,
Just over in the glory land;
Just over in the glory land,
There with the mighty host I'll stand,

Just over in the glory land.
"No bird," I'd whisper.
"Between us, you and me,
yes, things are okay."

In the times
he lingered quietly
between ether and earth,
possibly in that firmament
of his past
with a carousel
of fair-skinned
young women, cool
in organdy dresses
on warm Sunday afternoons,

I stared at some charity's
floral calendar
tacked to his wall,
noticed once more
his penchant
for circling, along
with family birthdays,
what seemed
such funny dates:
Greek Orthodox Easter,
Yom Kippur, Professional
Secretaries' Day.

A widower for years,
and still
he'd starred Valentine's
under February's floribunda.
Month after petaled month,
the one brightness left,
except for our last
shimmering glances
when we were almost
father and son.

MELANCHOLY

One quantum leap
from its dim world to our
guardian lamps
flooding garage doors
and beds
of anemones,
gloomy jogs of houses,
out toward
the ramble
of a thicket's edge,
and this
phosphorescent dervish of Luna
is stirring itself
into a living
sacrifice.

The televangelist I've muted
is begging
for deliverance of every
sin-sick soul,
that each blinded eye
should be fixed
on Christ,
deliverance perhaps even
from my own
bittersweet bondage
to moonlit spruce,
the waft
of polecats passing,
a nightjar's swift drumming
of wings,

and the apple-green fetish
of moth
swirling under
a white-hot mercy,
barely resisting some clarion call
to be transformed,
to finally be filled with
enough light,
till every realm
becomes intolerable
but one, where,
like a swallow-tailed phoenix,
it ascends and explodes
into incandescent
bliss.

GOLDEN YEARS

Better days must circle
heads like tarnished halos,
even at those special times
when another octogenarian
sits in the rec room
before candlelit cake
as if watching a house burn.

By all odds, pills
shouldn't have worked,
brakes should've failed,
or hearts simply stopped.
Instead, it's come to this:
air streaked with urine;
rewards of enemas
and ice cream; questions
of why the end
is taking so long.

Till then, Sundays
with their chatter
from kin about who
was at church,
rhododendrons in bloom,
remain odysseys for her
warmly shawled, fixed
by a silent piano,
lost in knit and purl,
odysseys for one mumbling
tongues in the corner,
and for two others hunched
over a checkerboard.

A FABLE

On a shallow of the frozen lake,
in a heap as white as gardenias,
a whooping crane lay oblivious
to sun-glistened snow, the murder
of crows floating in like braille.
When two white feathers tumbled
across the ice, I imagined a heart
fluttering to rise with the others
till their healthy trumpet
was more distant than stars.

And then, seemingly out of
nowhere, as if an answer
or ignoring of prayer,
a coyote rumbling with hunger,
rushed in to survive. As the crane
tore its frail beauty loose time
and again, almost taking flight,
for one scintillant moment
I thought I understood
the meaning of life.

STAPLES

Bread or aspirin,
or whatever desire
had me out so late,
brought me to him
waiting at his Bethesda,
not asking alms,
nor to be dipped
that the buds of his legs
might be restored,
but for a six-pack
of Busch talls.

Outside the store,
as I hand him his change,
he tells me he goes by
"Frank in the wheel chair,"
that he likes zydeco and jazz.

I tell him I teach
at the university,
ask if there's
anything more he needs,
wishing he'd confess
some hope to have
an incorruptible body,
share everlasting wealth,
and then, we send hosannas
to the lambent vault.
"Nope," he says smiling
and patting his sack,
"just a buzz . . .
like everyone else."

IDEA OF BEAUTY

In the end, all their sweetest dreams are Greek
to us imagining the dusky rooms
of khrusallid filled by visions of blooms
exquisitely plumped with nectar they'll seek
after emerging still crumpled and weak,
of fluttering through the florid perfumes
of joe-pye, butterfly weed—what one assumes
they've thirsted for week after cloistered week.

How could anyone guess that once they're done
warming, corymbs of candytuft wouldn't be
alpha and omega fanning their lust, that
the twinkle of a lovelier notion
riddles those compound eyes? What's heavenly
in rancid scraps, a rotting pomegranate?

MUSIC

There's no telling
   what it actually is—
      some clash,
         some melding, some

vibrato of throats,
   like a gift of tongues
      from the dusky grove,
         weaving through twilight,

between locust
   and oak
      till planted
         evening after evening

in the dull garden
   of my ears.
      If it's not
         a nightingale's horny serenade,

nor variation
   by our usual
      collage
         of insects,

and if it's not
   the theophany
      I've tried to suppose—
         then something, certainly something.

MOURNING SONG

It begins like a tear,
as much glory as despair
on the broken note.
Complete mystery drifts

from nearby timber or brush,
and under favored lintels,
falls imperceptibly over
chambers of dream.

Then, the world clears
again in that loveliest
of moments when one
is first released

from sleep and wakes
to think *dove . . .*
I'm alive . . . it's a dove
calling from the brink!

THE ONSLAUGHT OF SPRING

How much
lemon fluorescence
of forsythia
can you bear,
or a magnolia's
full pink effect
against billowing
slate blue sky,

how many emerald stems
of jonquils
risen like lust
over the still
sleeping grass?
How pungent must
the scent of bulbs
be this year?

What vast pandemonium
of the quick,
the rufous-breasted,
the pollen-gold birds
need return this time
before you grasp
of how little
use you are?

THE PERSISTENCE OF MEMORY

Decades past his power to zip
a tight spiral, yet whenever
our quarterback spots me,
after news of his latest divorce
and most recent companion,
he asks if I remember
our winning touchdown.

Nowadays, before I can smile
or nod, he's already onto
how after snagging his perfect bullet,
I was hit by the secondary,
swarmed in a moment by
their whole defense, and how
Bonehead Pye, our other receiver,
spun from his pattern, streaked
across the field and plowed underneath
an interminable tilting pile
to pull me free before
my knee touched ground.

Here is where I would have
the legend end, between
my forward progress and going down.
I'd stay there in the midst
of forearms like shivs
and them low bridging my legs,
in a more tangible misery
than the rose-colored dreams
with girls who were younger then
than our children are.

How can I tell him
I'm finding my own, different way
by the adoration of marsh flowers,
in hazy sunsets, that the best
of our best times are only
like Dali's wilting watches?

So what I do is offer
my sufficient grace of
"Hell yeah, we were smoking!"
for perhaps the last thing
on earth that he truly loves:
the part of the story where
we break loose down the sideline,
with stiff arms ready,
just Bonehead and me dashing
stride for stride into eternity.

SUMMER'S END

With
overripe berries
and the last
margin of wildflowers
and gauzy-winged dragonflies
skimming
a creek into
shimmering rings
above minnows
as bright as dimes,
our world seems
splendid, immutable.
Leaf by leaf,
the stream is laced
with green going to yellow and red
twirling
from a colonnade
of trees,
down
on stripes of light.
Near water
urging over mossy rubble,
it's hard to accept
that it's all
ending.
Parents have died,
and children are leaving.
Even the birds
ounce their singing,
begin flitting
to cover for night.
And under
the late glow of sun,
every place
whispers
that it's time

to move on,
that autumn must come,
autumn must come,
must come.

PARABLE, LATE OCTOBER

Sunny undulations of butterflies all along I-40
          outside Jackson, Tennessee,
fluttered above, at times in front of noon traffic.

          Belched from
the stripped stalks of truck farms,
          metamorphoses rose

and dipped, sylphidine, through bell-clear air
          toward their new Canaan
of flowers. Every few hundred yards, they arced

          eighteen-wheelers,
salesmen chasing quotas, and me dodging
          the gossamer wings,

as if I were in harmony with sawing fiddlers
          on a bluegrass station
I'd picked up between towns, headed for the hospital

          in Memphis again
where my mother lolled on painkillers,
          had gone weeks

without solid food. Empty myself, unable to hold
          a night's thin soup,
I thought of Thanksgiving and Christmas approaching,

          our two times of indulgence,
remembered how even in years as lean as bone,
          she adorned our table

from dented tins marked "Crisco" and "flour,"
          from a full day spent
seasoning maw, whatever collards we'd gleaned

before caterpillars and frost.
You wonder, don't you, if there could ever be
perfect joy in anything

this fragile, always straddling benevolence?
Then, as if blood rain,
her life flooded over me, the way in autumn,

she'd sit on the porch
and watch our garden unscroll in a flourish
of yellow,

and with solemn disgust tell us,
"Them o butterflies
done ruined the little greens," just as one,

the color of fool's gold,
failed like stuttered prayer—a thumbnail flick
against my windshield,

sublime blossom of crimson, violet and bronze,
resplendent paradigm
revealing what the kingdom of heaven is like.

HOPE AGAINST HOPE

For weeks, I kept my eye
on a windowpane, the rosette
of eggs left by a callow moth
too near our first cold snap.

I watched them turn through
hoarfrost and wind-chill,
from sheer chalcedony
to the umber of dirt,

not to find out how life worms
its way into light, if they'd
be appleleaf or death's-head,
sweetheart or emerald,

but for no reason other
than to see if anything
so utterly dead could
somehow rise and fly.

JOY IN THE MORNING

New Year's Eve, beginning
and ending within minutes
of each other, while snow
sifts through the dark.
From an upstairs window,
a body feels perched over
his own little world,
watching cedars, a peony bed,
lawn after flaxen lawn
being erased with white,
solemnly watching every
house without light
where couples finger
flutes of champagne,
snuggle by fire before
twelve o'clock's kiss,
or at least in the mind's eye.

Other than the moan
of a blues playing downstairs
and from outside, the slight
tick of ice, there's no sign
of life—no cottontails
flashing from the hedge,
nor a young raccoon
that holes up in
the fork of a dying yew,
not the neighbor's tabby
or even deer on a night
so perfectly made
for deer to punch
their clue into snow.

Just after midnight though,
bunches of crimped stems
along a windrow become

topiary of herons
about to take wing
from this history of aches,
toward morning that will be
void and without form,
ready to re-create.

WORDS TO LIVE BY

The days of our lives are seventy years; and if by reason of strength they are eighty years, yet their boast is only labor and sorrow; for it is soon cut off, and we fly away.
—PSALM 90:10

Unless you're in love
with the beauty of granite,
the touch of marble
chiseled to perfect corners,
dressed to handsome curves,
you can't fully value
lines like Gray's
"The paths of glory
lead but to the grave."

You have to have spent time
holding the palette of sunrise
in your sight, listening
as each kind of bird
begins its day,
watching them wing
from limb to limb
in the shining irony
of nothing truly new,
feeling the sun raise
hardly more than itself,
the first lively birds
and the bowed head
of a lily or two.

You must've sat
oblivious to traffic
on the road beyond—
drivers trying to get somewhere,
then somewhere else,
getting lost, running

out of gas. You must've sat
quietly by depressions of earth,
and with chalk and paper,
made rubbings of pearly gates
and cherubs hovering
like sentinels, of doves
with peace twigs
dangled from their beaks,
and mellifluous verses set
over the multitude of faults.

Among rows of crosses
as white and persistent
as morning light,
you could worry yourself
into despair as deep
as that Gadarene, whose demons
Jesus flung into swine.

For here lies the miser
who scrimped away
the desert of his life
trying to gain a world,
so much so that
what you see beyond
his middling obelisk
and a few sprigs of mint
inching over his plot,
is the lesson
of Dives and Lazarus,
or Mark's Gospel picturing the rich
as loaded camels struggling
to enter a needle's eye.

Here also is the once comely woman
for whom one sugar daddy

wasn't enough, then too many
when in their stormy
waters of love,
jealousy overflowed, fulfilled
an old blues prophecy,
and "let some graveyard
be her restin' place."

Below darting birds
and a sham of geraniums,
suffering kudzu's infernal greed,
children are here—
here, where you can only imagine them
sustained by umbilicals
of bright, swaying kites, or lost
in a land of make-believe.

Stories rise by turns
as wails of one praying
forgiveness or indulgence
for a cache of sin,
stories like that last
brief, unutterable message
from my uncle's jaundiced eyes.

Headstones appear like the sails
of tiny ships riding
swells of moss and crabgrass.
Everywhere, our frailty
is firmly carved. A quarter life
here, half a life there,
even the full eighty years
at end must seem no more
than a breath:
the outset of heartburn,
less spasms of the flesh,

and then, the unavoidable
road of descent.

Yet there's comfort
beyond every pain here:
in the mole that still enjoys
its pitch-dark work;
a spider launching itself
on a thread of faith;
in the thought of funerals
that have a second line
where dirges are jazzed
with resurrection tempo, parasols
and handkerchiefs erupt
in blossoms of promise,
and the procession, as if
kissing off death, sashays
the rest of their way.

Watching dusty light
bend through elm, shadow
crossing now and forever,
you find yourself
gleaning redemption from
a strength in words—
their grace, their heft.

Once during a most ordinary speech,
I'd drifted onto the path
toward a riverbank, absence,
perhaps into the pink clouds
of an impressionist painting
till I was brought back
to the speaker's voice,
found myself one
with his wedge of geese.

Being a man of science,
he went on about
their skill in flight,
how geese tend their sick,
mate for life—
all wonders I'd long known.
Then, in language
so lovely in its gist,
he began, "If we're serious
about why we're here," and paused
while his words settled over us.

"If we're serious
about why we're here"—
their sum of such
that I considered *work* and *regret*
and the bonding of geese,
how much power
is needed for each.

Just the whisper
of certain consonance
can lighten a walk
through ashes or violets,
help you appreciate bees
as they soak themselves
in honeysuckle thrill.

Some days I marvel
at how nature
is made to provide,
and I remember myself
searching the woods
like a treasury
for rainbow feathers,
a tang of muscadines,

finding the hapless, furry shell
returning to earth.

When my hunts were fruitless
except for clouds of honeysuckle,
I could sometimes steal
their sweet threads
even in lush humming,
without rousing a bee.

Maybe there's no better place
for everything to begin again
than among some asters
and purpling berries,
under the heaven
of robins' eggs,
no finer words
in any hymn than those
of "that great gettin' up morning"
when bodies break free,
escape death as if waking
from a dream to behold
what we've earned,
names are called
from celestial reams,
while we, so joyful,
by some form of wings, might
circle another magnificent world,
then like parched bees,
immerse ourselves in
the New Jerusalem.

SELAH

Autumn catches like wildfire, and I
            think of them,
Don and Frank, one hardly mentioned

            without the other,
each at his house, cleaning breechblocks,
            checking shot

till something was in season again.
            Camos were pulled
out like dusty religions, shaken,

            examined for tears.
I think of that first clear, frosty
            morning

coming each year, and them heading out,
            bringing in and placing
on a yellow kitchen table food to be

            plucked or skinned.
I hated being there in the evening
            after our cousin

Frank had claimed his share and left
            for home, when
my uncle took the butcher knife

            and made his split
across the back of whatever, then
            slipped its pelt

over shoulders and thighs, opened
            a creature
reduced to ribbons of crimson

to flip innards
in a pail. Next day, the same trails,
        the same talk

of craps rolling cold on someone
            at Jessie's
or Frank James', talk of

        a lost chance
with their perfect woman long ago,
        a sip of rye,

the luck of dogs jumping game.
        Anyone could tell
how much they liked listening to

        the music of hounds,
watching pointers freeze before a maze
        of brush.

But I wonder if either of them
            ever gave thanks
for the creamy splendor of sycamores

        freeing themselves,
islands of clouds, or for the psalms
        of their lives.

With stock to shoulder, together they
        waded through tides
of Johnson grass as seasons came

        and changed—
spring and summer with not much to do
        but sit outside,

joking while woodpeckers hammered
        into eaves of barns,
or perhaps stroll back through pines

        to the pond
caroling with frogs, for its occasional,
        gleaming strikes

of crappie and bream, and then
        fall again,
as if there just for them.

        Ten, fifteen years
after Don, I can still see him
        starting a quiet day,

sitting on that slab porch, it
        and his khakis,
flecked with tobacco spit, still hear

        Frank saying,
"I just can't believe Babeman Wilkinson dead,"
        when he and a friend

dropped by one misty afternoon with the last
        rabbits he'd bring,
still hear my mother saying, "Frank sure

        seemed hurt."
All the suns that rose and set
        without the crack

of guns in our woods seemed
        like the end
of them both till word came

that Frank
was surrendering his herculean
weight,

the strength from his legs
to a tingle,
he complained, like that of crawling grass

he'd felt
on so many hunts in many fields
before, the kind

that could somehow work its way
into boots,
climb calves and vex knees,

find one's
very heart given enough
time.

A few weeks later, we heard
he too was gone.
Now, in another of those heavens

we make
for ourselves, I keep them having passed
a purling brook,

just coming upon some golden rise
where a covey
booms into quilted skies.

DOXOLOGY AND BENEDICTION

May the meditation of our hearts
through joy or sorrow be full
and acceptable like the silence
of clouds; let us be one band,

obedient and redeemed, perfect
like the orchid or hawk, our
praise as beneath any verdant cliff
where the floods rise and clap hands.